The Gospel Of Peter

Bernhard Pick

Kessinger Publishing's Rare Reprints

Thousands of Scarce and Hard-to-Find Books
on These and other Subjects!

- Americana
- Ancient Mysteries
- Animals
- Anthropology
- Architecture
- Arts
- Astrology
- Bibliographies
- Biographies & Memoirs
- Body, Mind & Spirit
- Business & Investing
- Children & Young Adult
- Collectibles
- Comparative Religions
- Crafts & Hobbies
- Earth Sciences
- Education
- Ephemera
- Fiction
- Folklore
- Geography
- Health & Diet
- History
- Hobbies & Leisure
- Humor
- Illustrated Books
- Language & Culture
- Law
- Life Sciences

- Literature
- Medicine & Pharmacy
- Metaphysical
- Music
- Mystery & Crime
- Mythology
- Natural History
- Outdoor & Nature
- Philosophy
- Poetry
- Political Science
- Science
- Psychiatry & Psychology
- Reference
- Religion & Spiritualism
- Rhetoric
- Sacred Books
- Science Fiction
- Science & Technology
- Self-Help
- Social Sciences
- Symbolism
- Theatre & Drama
- Theology
- Travel & Explorations
- War & Military
- Women
- Yoga
- *Plus Much More!*

We kindly invite you to view our catalog list at:
http://www.kessinger.net

formance of certain prescribed acts He opposed the doing of the truth, which both the Fourth Gospel (III, 21) and the First Epistle of St. John (I, 6) represents, as the first condition of life in Christ. No mere acts in fastings, prayer, and almsgiving, no formal observance of external duties could secure the Divine reward, which depends on the assimilation and fulfilment of the Truth itself." (Expository Times, August, 1904, p. 493.)

X. REMAINS OF THE GOSPEL OF PETER.

1. *Patristic Notices.*

a. (The citizens of Nazareth) thought that he was the son of Joseph and Mary. But some say, basing it on a tradition in the Gospel according to Peter, as it is entitled, or "the book of James," that the brethren of Jesus were sons of Joseph by a former wife, whom he married before Mary.

Origen, *Comment. in Matt.* X, 17.

b. The Nazorites are Jews who revere Christ as a righteous man and use the so-called gospel according to Peter.

Theodoret., *Hær. fab. comp.* II, 2.

c. As to what are called his (i. e., Peter's) Acts, and the Gospel according to Peter, and that called "the Preaching and the Revelation of him," we know nothing of their being handed down as Catholic writings. Since neither

among the ancient nor the ecclesiastical writ-
ers of our own day, has there been one that
has appealed to testimony taken from them.

Eusebius, *Hist. Eccles.* III, 3, 2.

3. There is also another work composed by him
(i. e., Serapion)[1] on the gospel of Peter, as it
is called, which, indeed, he wrote to refute
the false assertions which it contains, on account of some in the church of Rhossus, who
by this work were led astray to perverted doc-
trines. From which it may be well to add
some brief extracts by which it may be seen
what he thought of the book: —

"We, brethren, receive Peter and the other
Apostles as Christ Himself. But those writings which falsely go under their name, as we
are well acquainted with them, we reject, and
know also, that we have not received such
handed down to us. But when I came to you,
I had supposed that all held the true faith; and
as I had not perused the gospel presented to
them under the name of Peter, I said 'If this
be the only thing that creates difference among
you, let it be read'; but now having under-
stood, from what was said to me, that their
minds were enveloped in some heresy, I will

---

[1] Serapion, Bishop of Antioch 190–203, on entering his see,
learned that there was a gospel attributed to Peter read in
the sacred services of the church of Rhossus, in Cilitia. He
at first sanctioned its use, but after a more careful examina-
tion Serapion regretted his precipitation in sanctioning the
use of the Gospel, and wrote a book upon it, "in refutation
of its false assertions."

make haste to come to you again; therefore, brethren, expect me soon. But as we perceived what was the heresy of Marcion, we plainly saw that he ignorantly contradicted himself, which things you may learn from what has been written to you. For we have borrowed this gospel from others, who have studied it, that is, from the successors of those who led the way before him, whom we call Docetæ (for most opinions have sprung from this sect). And in this we have discovered many things superadded to the sound faith of our Saviour; some also attached that are foreign to it, and which we have also subjoined for your sake."

Eusebius, *Hist. Eccles.* VI, 12, 2–6.

This was all that was known of the Gospel of Peter till the publication of the Akhmîm fragment which was discovered by the French Archæological Mission, Cairo, in a grave (supposed to be a monk's) in an ancient cemetry at Akhmîm (Panopolis) in Upper Egypt in 1886. It was published in 1892 under the care of M. Bouriant in the "Memoirs of the French Archæological Mission at Cairo," Vol. IX., fasc. i. The same parchment which contained this fragment also contained a fragment of the Revelation of Peter and a fragment of the book of Enoch in Greek.

The find soon produced a great literary activity, as can be seen from the bibliography.

The fragment begins in the middle of the history of the Passion, and ends in the middle of a sentence, with the departure of the disciples into Galilee at the end of the Feast of Unleavened Bread, exactly a week after the Crucifixion, the ostensible author, Peter, and Andrew, his brother, taking their nets and going to the sea.

The dependence of our Gospel upon the canonical gospels, especially the synoptical, is admitted by most scholars. It is also admitted that the Gospel of Peter was known to Justin. Harnack thinks that Clement of Alexandria, the Didascalia, Pseudo-Ignatius, Ephraem also perused the Gospel of Peter, and assigns as its date AC 110–130. It originated in Syria, but was also known in Egypt.

2. THE GOSPEL OF PETER.

I, 1. But of the Jews none washed his hands, neither Herod nor any of his judges. And when they had refused to wash them, Pilate rose up.

2. And then Herod, the King, commanded that the Lord be taken, saying to them: "What things soever I command you to do, do unto him."

II, 3. And there stood Joseph, the friend of Pilate and of the Lord, and knowing that they would crucify him, he came to Pilate, and asked the body of the

4. Lord for burial.— And Pilate sent to
5. Herod and asked his body.— And Herod said: " Brother Pilate, even if no one had asked for him, we should have buried him. For the Sabbath is drawing on; for it is written in the law, that the sun set not upon one that hath been put to death." And he delivered him to the people on the day before the feast of the unleavened bread, their feast.

III, 6. And they took the Lord and pushed him as they ran and said: " Let us drag away the Son of God, since we
7. have him in our power." And they clothed him with purple, and set him on the seat of judgment and said: " Judge righteously, O King of Israel."
8. And one of them brought a crown of thorns and put it on the head of the
9. Lord.— And others stood and spat in his eyes, and others smote his cheeks; others pricked him with a reed, and some scourged him, saying: " With this honor let us honor the Son of God."

IV, 10. And they brought two malefactors, and they crucified the Lord between them. But he held his peace, as though hav-
11. ing no pain. And when they had raised the cross they wrote the title: " This

12. is the King of Israel."— And having set his garments before him they parted them among them, and cast lots for

13. them.— And one of the malefactors reproached them and said: "We for the evils that we done have suffered thus, but this man, who hath become the Saviour of men, what wrong hath

14. he done to you?"— And they became angry at him and commanded that his legs should not be broken, that he might die in torment.

V, 15. And it was noon and darkness came over all Judæa, and they made a noise and were distressed, lest the sun had set, whilst he (Jesus) was yet alive. For it is written for them, that the sun set not on him that hath been put to

16, 17. death. And one of them said: "Give him to drink gall with vinegar." And they mixed and gave him to drink. And they fulfilled all things, and accomplished the sins against their own

18. head. And many went about with lamps, supposing that it was night, and fell down.— And the Lord cried out,

19. saying: "My power, my power, thou hast forsaken me," and after these

20. words he was taken up. And in that hour the vail of the temple of Jerusalem was rent in twain.

VI, 21. And then they drew out the nails from the hands of the Lord, and laid him

22. upon the earth.   And the whole earth quaked and great fear arose.— Then the sun shone, and it was found (that

23. it was) the ninth hour.— And the Jews rejoiced and gave his body to Joseph that he might bury it, since he had seen

24. what good things he had done.— And he took the Lord and washed him, and rolled him in a linen cloth, and brought him into his own tomb, called the Garden of Joseph.

VII, 25. Then the Jews and the elders and the priests, perceiving what evil they had done to themselves, began to beat themselves and to say: " Woe for our sins; the judgment has come nigh and the

26. end of Jerusalem."— And I with my companions was grieved, and being wounded in mind we hid ourselves. For we were being sought for by them as malefactors, and as wishing to set

27. fire to the temple.— And upon all these things we fasted and sat mourning and weeping night and day until the Sabbath.

VIII, 28. And the scribes and Pharisees and elders being gathered together one with another, when they heard that the whole people murmured and beat their breasts saying: "If by his death such great signs have taken place, see what right-

29. eous man he is."— And the elders were afraid and came to Pilate, beseeching

30. him and saying:—"Give us soldiers that we may guard his sepulchre for three days, lest his disciples come and steal him and the people suppose that he is risen from the dead and do us

31. evil."— And Pilate gave them Petronius the centurion with soldiers to guard the tomb. And with them elders and scribes went to the sepulchre,—

32. and with the centurion and the soldiers all who were there rolled a great stone and set it at the door of the

33. sepulchre,— and they affixed seven seals, and having pitched a tent there, they guarded it.

IX, 34. And when the morning of the Sabbath came, a multitude came from Jerusalem and the region round about, to see the

35. sealed sepulchre.— And in the night in which the Lord's day was drawing on, as the soldiers kept guard two by two, there was a great voice in the heaven,

36. — and they saw the heavens opened, and two men descending from thence with great splendor and coming to the

37. tomb.— That stone which was put at the door, rolled away of itself and made

way in part, and the tomb was opened and the two young men entered in.—

X, 38. And when the soldiers saw this, they awakened the centurion and the elders, for they too had remained there to keep

39. guard.— And as they were telling what they had seen, they saw again three men come forth from the tomb, and two of them supporting one, and a cross

40. following them,— and of the two the head reached into the heaven, but the head of him that was led by them over-

41. passed the heavens,— and they heard a voice from the heavens, saying: " Hast thou preached to them that sleep "—

42. And a response was heard from the cross: " Yea."—

XI, 43. They therefore considered one with another whether to go away and shew

44. these things to Pilate.— And while they yet thought thereon, the heavens again were seen to open, and a certain man to descend and enter into the sepulchre.

45. ulchre.— When the centurion and they that were with him saw these things, they hastened in the night to Pilate, leaving the tomb which they were watching, and declared all things which they had seen, being greatly distressed

46. and saying: " Truly He was the Son of God."— Pilate answered and said:

"I am pure from the blood of the Son of God; you have decided thus."—

47. Then they all drew near and besought him and entreated him to command the centurion and the soldiers to say nothing of the things which they had seen.

48. —"For it is better," say they, "to commit the greatest sin before God, and not to fall into the hands of the people

49. of the Jews and to be stoned."— And Pilate commanded the centurion and the soldier to say nothing.—

XII, 50. And at dawn upon the Lord's day, Mary Magdalen, a disciple of the Lord, fearing because of the Jews, since they were burning with wrath, had not done at the Lord's sepulchre the things which women are wont to do for their beloved

51. dead — she took her friends with her and came to the sepulchre where he

52. was laid.— And they feared lest the Jews should see them, and they said: "Although on that day on which he was crucified we could not weep and lament, yet now let us do these things

53. at His sepulchre.— But who shall roll away for us the stone that was laid at the door of the sepulchre, that we may enter in and sit by Him and do the things that are due?— For the stone was great, and we fear lest someone

54. see us. And if we cannot, yet if we but set at the door the things which we bring for a memorial of Him, we will weep and lament, until we come unto our home."

XIII, 55. And they went and found the tomb opened, and coming near they looked in there; and they see there a certain young man sitting in the midst of the tomb, beautiful and clothed in a robe exceeding bright, who said to them: —

56. "Wherefore are ye come? Whom seek ye? Him that was crucified? He is risen and gone. But if ye believe not, look in and see the place where he lay, that he is not (here); for he is risen and gone thither, whence he was

57. sent." Then the women feared and fled.—

XIV, 58. Now it was the last day of the unleavened bread, and many were going forth, returning to their homes, as the feast

59. was ended.— But the twelve disciples of the Lord wept and were grieved; and each one being grieved for that which was come to pass, departed to his

60. house.— But I Simon Peter and Andrew my brother took our nets and went to the sea; and there was with us Levi the son of Alphæus, whom the Lord . . .

Harnack (Texte und Untersuchungen IX, 2 (1893), has pointed out the following new traits contained in the Petrine account of the history of the Passion and burial:

1. Herod was the judge who condemned Jesus, and to him application had to be made for the body.

2. The Jews, Herod and the Judges would not wash their hands, and Pilate then raised the sitting.

3. Joseph was the friend of Pilate (II).

4. Joseph begged for the body before the crucifixion, and Pilate sent for permission from Herod.

5. The soldiers "pushed him as they ran" and their speech (III).

6. The mockery of the soldiers.

7. Mocking speech.

8. "As though having no pain" (IV).

9. "Having set his garments before him."

10. One of the malefactors blamed the multitude, and his speech.

11. The legs of either the malefactor or Jesus were not broken *that he might die in torment.*

12. The gall and the vinegar (V).

13. In the darkness many went about with lamps, and fell down.

14. The cry "My power, my power."

15. The fact that when he had so cried Christ was taken up.

16. Mention of the nails in the hands at the taking down from the cross (VI)
17. The earthquake when the body touched the ground.
18. The joy of the Jews when the sun shone again.
19. Joseph " had seen all the good things " that the Lord had done.
20. Joseph washed the body.
21. The cries of woe of the Jews and their leaders over their sins, and their expectation of the judgment on Jerusalem (VII).
22. The disciples remained in concealment, full of grief, and fasted and wept till the Sabbath.
23. They were searched for as malefactors and as anxious to burn the temple.
24. The name of the centurion of the watch — Petronius (VIII).
25. The centurion, the soldiers, and the elders rolled up the stone.
26. The elders also watched at the grave.
27. Seven seals were affixed to the stone.
28. A tent pitched for the watch.
29. The gathering of the multitude on the morning of the Sabbath to see the sealed sepulchre (IX).

The narrative of the resurrection also differs from that of the canonical gospels, as the reader can see for himself.

This is the end of this publication.

Any remaining blank pages are for our book binding
requirements and are blank on purpose.

To search thousands of interesting publications like this one,
please remember to visit our website at:

http://www.kessinger.net

CPSIA information can be obtained at www.ICGtesting.com

261177BV00004B/204/P